Bernadette Soubirous

Blessed Are the Pure of Heart

1844–1879

Born in Lourdes, France

Feast Day: April 16

Patron of the Sick and the Poor

"Blessed are the pure of heart
for they shall see God."
Matthew 5:8

Text by Barbara Yoffie
Illustrated by Chris Sharp

Liguori Publications
A Redemptorist Ministry

Dedication

To my family:
my parents Jim and Peg,
my husband Bill,
our son Sam and daughter-in-law Erin,
and our precious grandchildren
Ben, Lucas, and Andrew

To all the children I have had the privilege
of teaching throughout the years.

Imprimi Potest:
Kevin Zubel, CSsR, Provincial
Denver Province, the Redemptorists

Published by Liguori Publications, Liguori, Missouri 63057
To order, visit Liguori.org or call 800-325-9521.
Copyright © 2024 Liguori Publications

All rights reserved. No part of this publication may be reproduced, stored in a retrieval system, or transmitted in any form or by any means—electronic, mechanical, photocopy, recording, or any other—except for brief quotations in printed reviews, without the prior written permission of Liguori Publications.

ISBN (print): 978-0-7648-2866-9
ISBN (digital): 978-0-7648-7249-5

Liguori Publications, a nonprofit corporation, is a ministry of the Redemptorists.
To learn more about the Redemptorists, visit Redemptorists.com.

Printed in the United States of America
28 27 26 25 24 / 5 4 3 2 1
First Edition

Dear Parents and Teachers:

Saints and Me! is a six-set series of children's books about saints, including: *Saints of North America* who served our homeland; *Saints of Christmas*, who teach us to love Jesus; *Saints for Families*, who modeled God's love within and for the domestic Church; *Saints for Communities*, who served Jesus through various roles and professions; and *Saints for Sacraments*, who showed great love for the sacraments.

The eight books in *Saints of the Beatitudes* (a word meaning "a list of blessings from God") introduce nine holy people who exemplify attributes Jesus articulated in his Sermon on the Mount. Faustina Kowalska's diary *Divine Mercy in My Soul,* read by millions, helped spread God's message of mercy. Patrick, a missionary, brought Christianity to Ireland. Monica prayed her wayward son, Augustine, would return to the faith. He did and was canonized. Katharine Drexel abandoned her comfortable life to become a nun. Carlo Acutis shared his faith and love of the Eucharist through technology. Bernadette Soubirous experienced visions of the Blessed Virgin Mary. Pope John XXIII convoked the Second Vatican Council, hoping to revive the Church. Jude was an apostle of our Lord.

Which saint was captured by pirates and sold into slavery? Name the saints with back-to-back feast days (August 27–28). Who gave $20 million to build churches and schools? Who created a website about eucharistic miracles? Who did Jesus appear and speak to? Who said, "My job is to inform, not to convince"? Who wrote *Peace on Earth* in 1963? Who is the patron of impossible causes? Find out in the *Saints of the Beatitudes* set—part of the *Saints and Me!* series—and help children connect to the lives of the saints.

Introduce your children or students to *Saints and Me!* as they:

—**READ** about the lives of the saints and are inspired by their stories.

—**PRAY** to the saints for their intercession.

—**CELEBRATE** the saints and relate them to their lives.

Free activities for children to use with this book may be downloaded at Liguori.org.

The Beatitudes

Divine blessings Jesus names in his Sermon on the Mount

Matthew 5:3–12

Saints of the Beatitudes

Patrick

Blessed Are the Poor in Spirit (Verse 3)

Monica and Augustine

Blessed Are They Who Mourn (Verse 4)

Katharine Drexel

Blessed Are the Meek (Verse 5)

Carlo Acutis

Blessed Are the Righteous (Verse 6)

Faustina Kowalska

Blessed Are the Merciful (Verse 7)

Bernadette

Blessed Are the Pure of Heart (Verse 8)

Pope John XXIII

Blessed Are the Peacemakers (Verse 9)

Jude the Apostle

Blessed Are the Persecuted (Verses 10–12)

Bernadette was a quiet little girl who loved God. When she was fourteen years old, God chose her to bring his message of love to the world. The Virgin Mary appeared to Bernadette eighteen times with messages of prayer and penance. Bernadette followed God's plan for her life with a loving and pure heart.

Her family lived in Lourdes, a village in southern France near the mountains. They were very poor and lived in a dark basement with hardly any furniture. Bernadette was sick a lot and often missed school. But she was happy and loved to help with chores, like watching her younger brothers and sisters, cooking with her mother, and gathering firewood.

One day, she was playing with her sister and a friend in a grassy meadow. It was Bernadette's turn to find firewood. "Will you help me?" she asked her sister. "Sure, follow us!" The girls ran toward the river. "Wait for me!" Bernadette shouted.

Suddenly, she heard a strange noise. Then she saw a bright light. A beautiful lady appeared in the opening of the small cave (or grotto) where Bernadette was standing. The lady wore a long white dress and a veil on her head. A blue sash was tied at her waist, and yellow roses lay at her feet. She held a rosary in her hand. Bernadette stared at the lady and slowly walked toward the grotto.

Frightened at first, Bernadette knelt down and took her rosary out of her pocket. She started praying the rosary, and when she finished, the lady smiled at her and disappeared. Bernadette closed her eyes. She was not afraid anymore. She felt peaceful and happy.

Just then, her sister and friend came running toward her. “Bernadette, where were you?” they asked.

“I was right here. Did you see the lady in the grotto?”

“No, but we found lots of firewood. We better go home now.” As they walked across the meadow, Bernadette told them about the beautiful lady.

As soon as they got home, Bernadette's sister told their parents what happened at the grotto. "Oh, Bernadette, that's a silly story," said her mother. "But it's the truth," Bernadette sighed.

That night, Bernadette could not fall asleep. She kept thinking about the lady with the rosary. *"Tomorrow, I am going back to the grotto!"* she thought. And she did!

Bernadette went to the grotto to see the lady many times. Sometimes they prayed together. Other times, the lady gave her messages or asked her for help. Bernadette was happy to do whatever the lady wanted her to do.

During the third visit, the lady asked Bernadette, "Would you please come back to see me for the next fifteen days?" Bernadette answered, "Yes, of course!" A few days later, the lady told her to pray for sinners, people who have turned away from God. "Do penance. Do small things to make up for the sins of others."

Neighbors and people in town wondered what was happening at the grotto. A big crowd followed Bernadette. They watched her as she stared at an empty space in the grotto. Some people thought she was seeing a vision from God. Others thought she was making up stories. They asked, "What is wrong with Bernadette?"

Then one day, the lady told her, “Dig in the dirt and drink the water from the small spring.” Bernadette looked around but did not see a spring. The lady pointed to a rock. Bernadette started digging until she reached a small puddle of water. She tried to take a drink but got mud on her face instead! People laughed at her!

Everyone was surprised the next day when they saw the water. It was clear and fresh! It trickled down in a little stream. People drank and touched the water because they thought something wonderful would happen. Soon, miracle cures took place at the spring!

Many people came to Lourdes to see if the miracles were true. The leaders in the village did not know what to do! Church leaders were worried, too! They asked Bernadette lots of questions. "I am only telling you what I see and hear," she replied.

Bernadette talked to her parish priest, saying, "Father, the lady wants a chapel built near the spring." "Do you know the lady's name?" he asked. Bernadette shook her head, "No, Father." "Tell me her name and I will help you," he promised

Bernadette asked the lady her name many times. Finally, on March 25, the lady told Bernadette, "I am the Immaculate Conception." Bernadette repeated the words to herself and hurried to tell her parish priest. He was so surprised! The Immaculate Conception is another name for the Virgin Mary. The beautiful lady in the grotto was Mary, the Mother of God!

Crowds of people visited the grotto hoping to see the Virgin Mary or talk to Bernadette about her visions. She was polite and answered their questions.

A few years after the visions stopped, Bernadette became a nun. It was quiet in the convent, where she could pray and help the sick. During this time, she got sick, too. But she was cheerful, and did not complain.

Bernadette died on April 16, 1879, while praying the rosary. Pope Pius XI canonized Bernadette on December 8, 1933, the feast of the Immaculate Conception. She is a saint in heaven because of her prayerful, holy, and humble life.

The grotto in Lourdes, where the Virgin Mary appeared to Bernadette, is now a popular Marian shrine and the site of many miracles.

Millions of people visit the shrine each year to pray for healing and to drink or wash in the water at Lourdes.

Mary loves her children and asks all of us to pray
For sinners, the sick, and the poor—every day.

Saint Bernadette,
You loved God with a pure heart.
Mary's visits brought you peace and joy.
May we love Mary just as you did
and follow your example of prayer,
humility, and obedience.
Amen.

GLOSSARY (NEW WORDS)

Canonized: When the pope declares a person a saint

Chapel: A small church

Convent: A house where a group of women religious live

Grotto: A small cave

Humble: Meek, modest; not thinking you are better than someone else

Humility: Being humble or acting in a humble way

Immaculate Conception: The teaching that Mary was free from original sin and remained sinless all her life

Miracle: A wonderful event that cannot be explained and that shows God's love for us

Penance: To do something that shows you are sorry for sins; a prayer for forgiveness

Shrine: A holy place that marks the spot of an event in a saint's life or a miracle

Spring: An underground source of water

Vision: Seeing someone or something that is hard to explain

Saints and me!

SAINTS FOR SACRAMENTS

Booklets in this set honored by the Association of Catholic Publishers!

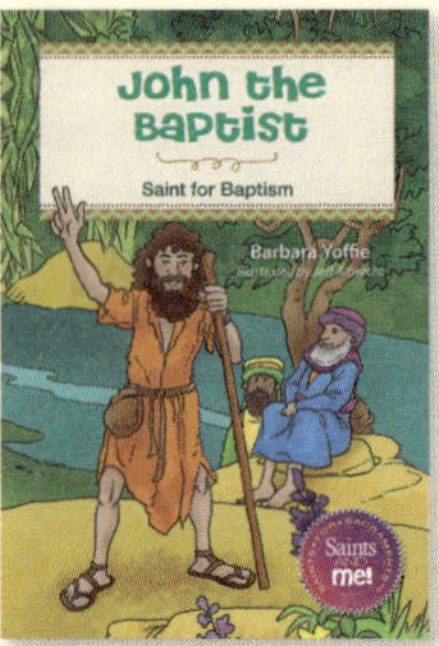

John the Baptist: Saint for Baptism 827969

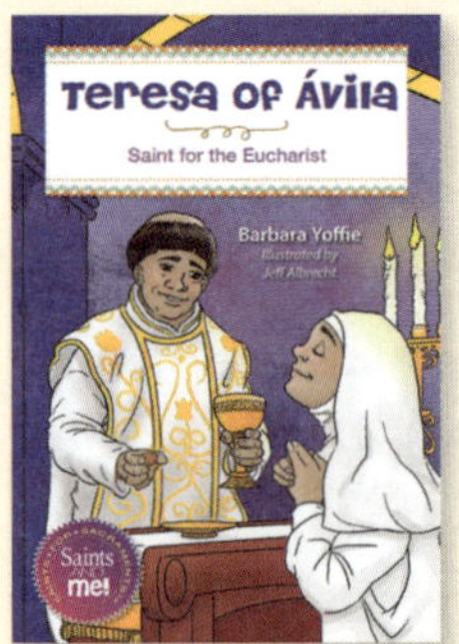

Teresa of Ávila: Saint for the Eucharist 827938

Padre Pio: Saint for Reconciliation 827921

Philip Neri: Saint for Confirmation 827976

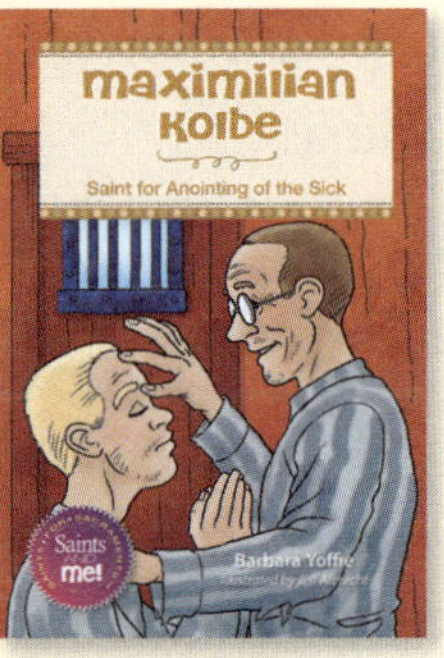

Maximilian Kolbe: Saint for Anointing of the Sick 827983

Louis and Zélie Martin: Saints for Matrimony 827945

John Vianney: Saint for Holy Orders 827952

Saints for Sacraments Activity Book 828010

Get the Complete Set!

Saints for Sacraments Collection A00085

(*Activity Book* sold separately)

Booklets: 32 pages, 5.5 x 8.5, Full-color illustrations

Activity Book: 96 pages, 8.5 x 11

Order today! Call 800-325-9521 or visit Liguori.org.

lonely planet

Western USA

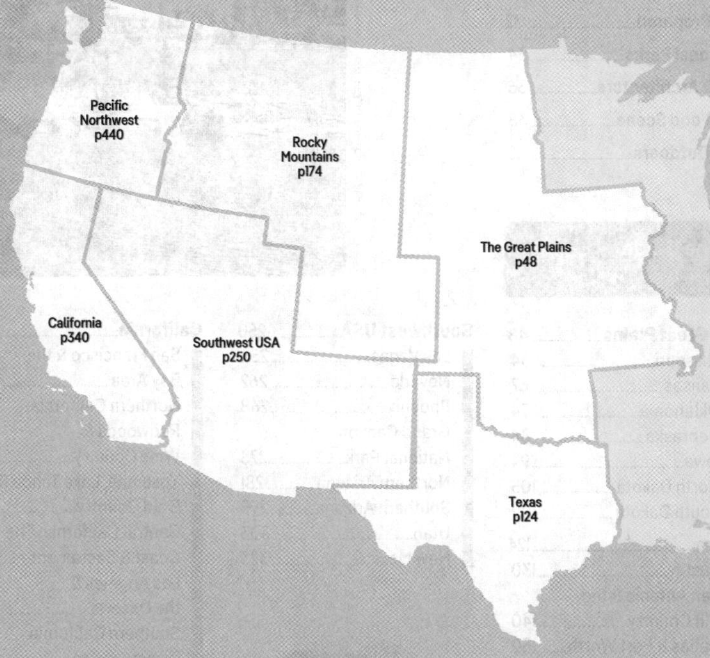

Amy C Balfour, Margot Bigg, Sarah Etinas, Anthony Ham, Lauren Keith, Amelia Mularz, Liza Prado, Helena Smith, Regis St Louis

CONTENTS

FROM LEFT: BENJAMIN HEATH FOR LONELY PLANET, SUZIE DUNDAS FOR LONELY PLANET, LIZA PRADO FOR LONELY PLANET

Plan Your Trip

The Guide

Seals, Fisherman's Wharf (p355), San Francisco